Saying Goodbye to My Evil Twin

NICOLE HAYES

authorHOUSE®

AuthorHouse™
1663 Liberty Drive
Bloomington, IN 47403
www.authorhouse.com
Phone: 833-262-8899

Published by AuthorHouse 12/04/2021

ISBN: 978-1-6655-4679-9 (sc)
ISBN: 978-1-6655-4678-2 (e)

Library of Congress Control Number: 2021924845

Print information available on the last page.

Any people depicted in stock imagery provided by Getty Images are models, and such images are being used for illustrative purposes only. Certain stock imagery © Getty Images.

This book is printed on acid-free paper.

CONTENTS

Chapter 1

MY CHILDHOOD

So, let me just begin. As far back as I can remember, my childhood was pretty normal. I lived with my mom, dad, and brother. Growing up, my father was an alcoholic. Actually, my father's side of the family were all alcoholics. I tried alcohol for the first time when I was fifteen years old. I used to put liquor in a small hairspray bottle and put it in my pocketbook to sneak it out of the house. Then, I would buy a water ice and mix it with the liquor. I was not a big fan of it, but I know it changed my way of thinking. That part I did like. For the next four years, I drank only when I wanted to drink to get drunk.

Chapter 2

MY EARLY TEENS

I found myself in a lot of messed-up situations. Guys tried to take advantage of me. I was almost raped. Money was stolen from me. My reputation was ruined because of it. Then, at the age of nineteen, I started hanging out with different friends and was introduced to marijuana for the first time. I started smoking cigarettes. By this time, my self-esteem was low—lower than it had ever been or I could have ever imagined. But when I smoked weed, I felt good. From that point on, I smoked pot every day, all day, and was a functioning pothead.

Chapter 3
THE WEED ERA

I smoked from the age of nineteen to thirty-one, except when I was pregnant with my two children. When I was around the age of twenty, we found out my father had been cheating on my mother for years, and he left. At this point I was smoking more weed and using Xanax with it. I was very upset over my father and what he'd done. He had no contact with my brother and me after he left, which really messed us both up mentally and emotionally. Also, during the eleven years of that time period, I was verbally, mentally, and emotionally abused by my children's father.

Chapter 4

ESCAPE FROM ABUSE

Well, I knew I was in a domestic violence situation. I had to get myself and my kids out of it before it turned into physical abuse. So I came up with a plan. I would go to nursing school, pass my boards, get a nursing job, and get myself and the kids out of the situation. The only problem was that I knew it was going to be hard and would take time. I was working, going to school, taking care of two kids, paying for everything, and pretty much running the house while their father was not there, high, or drunk.

That was when Percocet came into my life. I fell in love. I was about thirty-four years old. Those pills enabled me to stay up and do everything I had to do. However, my habit became too expensive to maintain. So, with the abuse going on and the expensive habit I now had, I packed up, took the kids, and moved to my mother's house.

Chapter 5

SOMEONE I THOUGHT I KNEW

Things seemed to be going well at first. I had a great nursing job, was living with my kids and my mom, was dating D, and was falling in love. It was wonderful—for a hot minute. Let's not forget I was using pills, and so was D. When we celebrated my thirty-fifth birthday, we had cake and eighty milligrams of OxyContin. At this point, we were snorting the pills. Things were getting real really quickly.

We ran out of money. I called nurses I used to work with and residents I used to take care of in a nursing home, trying to borrow money. I took money right out of the pocketbooks of people I worked with. Insane.

Then I decided I was going to steal checks from my mom. I took a lot. The pills turned me into someone I didn't even know. When Mom found out, I got kicked out of her house. I was living in my car and eating out of dumpsters. Then I was couch surfing and staying with people. At one point, I was using someone's closet as my bedroom. During this time, I missed a court date regarding custody for my kids because I was so sick. Around this same time, I missed my daughter's kindergarten graduation.

Chapter 6

HOMELESS

I became completely homeless because I had stolen from anyone who let me stay with them. As soon as they found out, I was kicked out.

I talked to a man at the welfare office who was helping me with food stamps. He was creepy. He wanted to take naked pictures of me for money. I told him no, that wasn't going to happen ever. He told me about a woman named Anne who rented out rooms. He gave me her number and told me to call and see if she had a room to rent. About the same time, D said, "You know, we can get fourteen bags of heroin for $120, and that would be more than if we bought Oxy eighties. They're the same thing."

I said, "OK, let's do it. Why didn't you tell me this before?"

Before that happened, I called Anne about renting a room. When I met with her, she said that D and I could rent the room and pay her $400 a month plus food to stay there. That's what we did. We had a place to stay, so we took our things and moved in.

Chapter 7

JOURNEY WITH HEROIN

Before I knew it, D and I were on our way to Kensington to buy heroin. At thirty-five years old, I found myself in Kensington without a job, renting a room from some woman I didn't even know.

Now we had to figure out how to support our habit. D was the only one working, and he only got paid on Fridays. My job became getting money every other day of the week so we would not be sick. I lied to everyone I knew, making up crazy stories to get money. Again I stole everything that I could pawn to make money. It was a full-time job to get $120 every day so that, by the time D was done working, we could go down to Kensington to get a bundle. I actually made more money than that every day, so I could go down without him and get a few bags for myself.

One day, D said he wanted to shoot heroin. I said, "If you do it, I'm doing it too." He said no at first, but I told him I was going to do it with or without him. It was his choice. Of course, I knew he would say he'd rather do it with me. We went and got works and some heroin, and we shot up. We were in love—not with each other, but with shooting heroin into our veins.

D also told me, "We can get cocaine and mix it with the heroin and shoot it together. It is called a speedball. You get a different high, but it is such a good high." So I tried that too; it was another love.

Chapter 8

SUPPORTING OUR HABIT

There were other people renting rooms where we were staying. I started stealing things from them. I took anything they had of value. I had my tax refund to use at one point and food stamps to sell. I had a restaurant that would buy half of my food stamps every month. I stole the rent money back from Anne. I knew where she put it, so when the other tenants paid her, and I would go take it. She knew someone in the house was stealing, but she had no idea who it was. She thought it was another girl and kicked her out. I broke into Anne's room and stole all her money and gold jewelry. I even figured out the PIN to her MAC and took money out of there several times.

I sold my car for $400, and Anne got us a new one so I could take D to work. We lied to her for months, saying D wasn't getting paid when actually he was. She gave him work or jobs around the house to make up for the rent we weren't paying her. When D got side jobs, I went with him and stole things from those people's houses. I even went so low as to steal from a church one time. We would lie to D's mother to get money. We would tell Anne that we needed help with court costs and fines, and she would help us so that we would not get locked up. In reality, we were using that money for drugs.

Chapter 9

COPPING OUR DRUGS

Every morning, I would drive D to work in the car Anne bought for us, and then go back to the house for a few hours to sleep. I would get up, get ready for the methadone clinic, and go to Kensington to get my drugs. See, at one point, I was trying to get clean because I wanted a healthy relationship with D. I would leave the clinic and immediately go to buy a couple of bags of heroin and sometimes a bag of coke too.

One time a guy took my thirty dollars (which, by the way, was all I had), came back, and gave me some crap. I think it was oregano. I was so mad that I went back looking for him with a baseball bat! Who does that?

Another thing that happened when I was by myself was I came back to my car after getting half my drugs, and there was a boot on my car. So I did the drugs I had, went and got the rest, and waited for the authorities to come remove the boot. That was a fun experience—not!

Two times, I got arrested down there. The first time, I was caught in a sting operation. I had no idea what a sting was until that day. D got out of the car, went into the dealer's house, and came back with the drugs. We drove away. As we were stopped at a traffic light, undercover officers ripped us out of the car and arrested us. I was in the Roundhouse overnight and was able to sign a ROR, because I was never arrested before. As for D, he was sent to CFCF for a couple of days. I had to pay his bail to get him out and then pick him up. He was very sick because he was going through withdrawal. Before I got him, I met one of our dealers and got a few bags for him.

The second time I got caught, I had actually been clean for six weeks. I went down with D to get three bags for him because he was sick. He waited in the car. After I got three bags, I got stopped by the cops. They found the heroin and arrested me. I was in the Roundhouse overnight and given a court date.

Chapter 10

KENSINGTON EXPERIENCE

*L*et me tell you a little about Kensington. You would not believe the things I have seen down there. I cannot believe the things I have seen. People fight each other over free samples, which are given out every Tuesday and Thursday mornings between five o'clock and eight o'clock in the morning, and sometimes on Sundays. I saw someone stab another person with a piece of glass over a sample. There is so much homelessness and people begging. Anything you can think of is going on. It's sad, but it's reality. You have to watch your back at all times.

I was desperate one day because I could not hit a vein. A Spanish guy I was cool with took me to a guy he knew in a shady place that was hidden, so this guy, whom I did not know, could shoot me up. I think back on that now, and I know they could have done anything to me. I mean, this place was a mobile home, in a lot behind a fence that was covered with leaves. No one knew I was there. They could have raped me or, even worse, killed me.

Chapter 11

TRYING TO GET CLEAN

One night, D and I were talking and crying to each other. I thought if I showed him that I could get clean, maybe he would try too. So, right then, I quit everything. Within hours I started going through withdrawal. The withdrawal hit hard, and I was extremely sick. Keep in mind I was going through withdrawal from heroin, cocaine, and methadone all at once. It lasted for six weeks. I lost a lot of weight. I weighed 118 pounds. I thought by doing that, I would give D incentive to stop. It did not work.

Chapter 12
FIRST RELAPSE

Obviously, quitting did not work. Because I was living with D, and D did not quit, it was only a matter of time before I started using again. I threatened it at first, thinking it would make him say, "No, babe, don't do it. I will quit too." However, that was not the case. After six weeks clean, I went back to using again.

At this time, we were putting shingles on Anne's garage roof to earn money to get our drugs. By the next day, I had a huge headache, was sore, and could barely walk. That was the last thing I remember before I woke up in Jefferson Hospital two months later.

Chapter 13
HOSPITAL STAY

Apparently, I had been so sick at Anne's house that I could not even go to the bathroom myself. D told me that he had to carry me there. I also found out he was shooting me up with drugs and leaving me for hours to walk down to Kensington and buy drugs. He was lying to my mother, saying he had taken me to the hospital when he had not.

He finally called my mother and told her the truth when he saw spots on my hands and feet. I was told my mother and brother came and got me right away and took me to the hospital. The doctors told them if they had not gotten me there when they did, I would not have woken up because my kidneys were shutting down. I basically had been dying in that bed at Anne's.

I had a few heart attacks and a couple strokes and was diagnosed with endocarditis. The doctor kept me on antibiotics for as long as he could, but he told the surgeon it was now or never because my heart was failing. I had to have open heart surgery with a double valve replacement and a pacemaker because I had knocked out the entire electrical system of my heart. They gave me a 5 percent chance of walking out of the hospital. They did not know how much brain damage I had, if any, from the strokes. They placed me in a medically induced coma.

When I finally woke up, I had to learn how to walk, talk, write, and eat all over again. Since then, I havehad another heart surgery in 2018 and another pacemaker surgery in 2020.

Chapter 14

SECOND RELAPSE

When I was released from the hospital and went home, I was clean and stayed clean for eight months. However, I could not wait to contact D. I missed him. So I called him, and he answered the phone. He was back living with his mom. He told me he was clean but on Suboxone. I was very happy and could not wait to see him.

Well, D lied. He was not clean. He was still using. I was upset. I begged him to please get help. I did not want him to die or go through what I had gone through. This time he agreed and went for treatment.

The sick part of all this is that he wasclean, and I had eight months clean—but then I relapsed. I hid it from everyone. We were out to dinner one night, and somehow my mom found out I was using again. She called D. That was it. He said it was over. He took me to detox, and immediately from there, he took me to a recovery house. You might have thought the hospital was my rock bottom, but it was not.

Chapter 15

RECOVERY HOUSE (THIRD RELAPSE)

$\mathcal{D}$ and my mom sent me to a recovery house in Croydon. What an experience that was. I was in a house of about ten women. We were each assigned certain chores weekly. We had to be out of the house every day from 8:00 a.m. until 3:00 p.m. We had to attend meetings in the house and out. We underwent random drug tests, and if a woman tested positive for anything, she was immediately kicked out, no questions asked. We also had a house manager.

It was okay at first, until a woman threatened to set me on fire. She was asked to leave. Then another woman started coming home drunk all the time. She was asked to leave. The house was becoming an unsafe environment, making it hard to stay clean.

Finally my roommate started coming home high on

heroin. I walked in on her doing it one night. Guess you know what happened next—I relapsed again. I was able to hide it. However, my roommate got caught and told on me.

I was out with a friend of mine, Adrian, and we were driving to meet up with some guys and go wave running. Both of our phones started ringing, and we were getting text messages. It was our house manager, Renee, telling us to come back immediately. I knew what was going on, but Adrian did not. I told her what was going on and warned her that Renee was going to want to drug test us as soon as we got back.

I tested positive, of course, and was told to leave right away. I packed all my things into Adrian's car and left. At that point, my only option was to call another friend of mine, Jess, who had been kicked out a few weeks earlier. I thought she could get me into the place where she was. She called back and said yes, so both Adrian and I went to live there. It was a sober house.

Chapter 16

SOBER HOUSE

After being in the sober house for a while, I met a couple named Barb and Mike. Mind you, I had never stopped getting high since my third relapse at the recovery house. I was able to hide it for a while. I even took the train and El one day all the way from Croydon to West Philly to buy drugs. The house manager never drug-tested me for weeks.

However, one day, I came in high on heroin and Xanax and passed out on my bed for four hours. Then she knew I was high. I was told to leave. I packed up and called my friend Sam, who is a doctor. He said he would pay for a hotel room for me until I figured out what to do. I feel bad that I used him for his money.

Chapter 17

HOTEL ROOM

$\mathcal{I}$ lived in the hotel room for weeks. Sam would come over, and we would smoke weed. Mike and Barb would pick me up. and we would go to West Philly or Kensington to get coke and heroin. Eventually my mom said I could come home, but I had to be clean. My plan became to use Suboxone for a little while so I could move back home.

Chapter 18

BACK HOME

I was back home and still using. Barb and Mike had a car, and so I would come up with the money. I breaking into houses. This went on for several months. If you think breaking into houses was bad, Barb was getting high every day, and she was pregnant. On top of using heroin, she was using Xanax and Klonopin. It made me sick every time she shot up.

I would sometimes meet a guy I knew from down the way, Jose, and we would take the bus together to cop our drugs. I did not know him that well, but I felt safe with him because he was Spanish and knew some people down there.

That is how I met Jason. One day Jose and I were down there, and Jason came over and started talking to both of us. From that point on, Jason and I were friends.

We exchanged numbers and talked every day. We even hung out a number of times. I knew there was more than just friendship there, but we had to get clean before anything could happen, and we both knew that.

Also during this time, I hung out with Caroline, a woman I met at detox. We, of course, would get high together.

All of us were getting money any way that we could. My God, I even stole from my grandmother. My friends were stealing and pawning stuff, and Caroline was boosting. We were all doing illegal things. I knew it was just a matter of time until we went to jail.

Then my son found Caroline on the kitchen floor and called my mom. My uncle came to the house and told Caroline and me to leave. We went to a hotel, and that is where I lived for almost two months.

Caroline was disgusting. She had different men in there every other night, having sex with them while her kid was sleeping on the floor. She would take Xanax and drive down the boulevard. She would fall asleep, almost killing us, but she would not let me or anyone else drive.

After two months of all this crap, I begged my mom to once again let me come home. The same rules applied: I had to be clean to come back. Suboxone was again the plan to get me through the door.

Thank God, this whole time my mother had custody of my kids, because I could not even take care of myself. I do have to say that I did everything and anything to get money, but the one thing I never did was sell myself. I could never do that to myself or my kids.

Chapter 19

GETTING ARRESTED

One day, I was high at my mom's house, doing homework with my six-year-old daughter, and there was a knock on the door. It was the police with a warrant for my arrest. I thought I was going to die right there on the step. I told them who I was and let them in. Thank God, they were considerate of my daughter and let me call my mom to come home and be with her.

The police let me walk out, smoke a cigarette, and get in the back of an unmarked car. They did not handcuff me in front of my daughter. They called for a paddy wagon to meet us at the end of the block, so my daughter would not see anything. I am very thankful for that. I did not want her traumatized by the whole event.

I must say, the police in the paddy wagon were a lot less humane. One of them kept saying to me, "You are going away for a long time." For some reason, I knew in my heart that I was not. I also knew in my heart that God intervened there, took me off the streets, and sat me down for a while. If he had not, the lifestyle I was living would have killed me.

Chapter 20
SURVIVING JAIL

My experience in jail was crazy. It was nothing like spending a couple nights in the Roundhouse. That was a piece of cake compared to what I went through in jail. First off, I was in the minority, being a Caucasian woman. Second, I had no idea how things worked there. Third, it was a whole different world in there, or let me say it was a world of its own. I cannot believe the things I saw and went through there. If you are wondering, yes, there were several times I had to protect and defend myself. The only thing I looked forward to was mail from my family and my friend, Jason, and the commissary.

Going through withdrawal in there is terrible. It is cold, the beds are hard, and you have a cellmate as you are sick, constantly throwing up and having diarrhea. You cannot eat. You do not want to eat because the food is terrible anyway. The guards m you shower after a couple days, even though you are so sick and cannot move. Your whole body hurt. This was the worst experience of my entire life—although in a way it was the best, because I needed it to save my life.

In the beginning, I cried and begged my mother to please bail me out. After a couple weeks in, I told her to leave me there, and I would be fine. I did not want my kids or anyone to visit and see me like that. I did talk to my kids every night on the phone.

You know, they say at some point in your addiction, you have a spiritual awakening. Well, I remember that one day, I was in my cell by myself with nothing—no commissary, not a penny to my name, nothing. And it happened. I felt the Holy Spirit come into my heart. I know it sounds crazy, but it's true. That was all I needed to get through everything that I was going through. I knew everything was going to be all right. That was my life-changing moment. Getting arrested and thrown in jail was my rock-bottom and literally the thing that saved my life. While I was in jail, nineteen people who got released died of accidental overdoses.

The seven months I was in jail were extremely hard. I could not wait to see my kids. But, it was worth it in the end.

The first time I had court, no guards came to get me, so I had to wait a whole month to find out what my sentence would be. If you don't know much about how things work in jail, everything goes slowly, extremely slowly. The following month, I was scheduled for another court date. All I had available to wear was the clothes that I got arrested in, and boy did they smell like a hamper. It was disgusting. I had no makeup on, my hair was not done, my clothes were dirty, and I wore slippers. I had no choice.

My lawyer and other people ahead of my date in court told me to take whatever I got as long as immediate parole was read after it. My sentence was eleven and a half to twenty-three with immediate parole to FIR. I pled no contest to all my charges and took what they gave me. I was handcuffed and shackled and led back out. As soon as I left the courtroom and was by myself, I broke down crying. I did not want my mom to see me like that. I can't tell you how mentally hard that was on me.

Anyway, after all that, they took me back to jail, and I had to sit and wait to be released to the FIR program at Kirkbride Center, which is an inpatient rehab center. I waited for about three more months. Then I was finally handcuffed, shackled, and put into a paddy wagon at about seven o'clock in the morning to be driven to Kirkbride Center. That was a happy, beautiful day.

Chapter 21

INPATIENT REHAB BEGINS

I finally made it! My thirty days of inpatient rehab treatment began. You would have thought I had been sent to a five-star hotel by the way I was acting. It was amazing. They had soft beds with pillows, and awesome food you could actually eat. "You don't know what you got till it's gone"—that saying is so true. Those were just two small things. There were plenty more.

We had to attend meetings every day, a variety of types. We had speakers come in who were in recovery themselves. We had to meet with our counselors on certain days. We also had downtime when we were allowed to do yoga and Zumba. We had movie nights, when we were allowed to get together and hang out and play cards or other games.

I do have to be honest here. During my stay at

Kirkbride, my roommate started using Xanax. One night, she asked me to hide it for her. So I did. Bad move. I hid it in me, if you know what I mean. In the morning when I woke up, it was melted, and I was high.

I just said to everyone that I had relapsed. I stood up in the middle of the auditorium and apologized for it. As addicts, we have very impulsive and compulsive behaviors. The guilt and shame I felt because of what I had done was unbearable, and it was very hard to overcome. Not only had I let myself down, but I felt like I had let the entire facility down.

On top of all that, I had no idea what was going to happen to me. I did not know if I was going to be kicked out, sent back to jail, or, worse, sent upstate for five years. All I knew was that I had to apologize to everyone there.

Needless to say, I was not kicked out or sent back to jail. I finished my required thirty days and was released to home to begin my outpatient treatment at NHS. When I got home and knocked on the door, my mom knew I was coming, but my daughter did not. We were trying to surprise her. My mom let me in, and I bent down to give my daughter a hug. She would not come to me at first. She was scared of me. That was the worst feeling. It broke my heart. I told her that it was okay and to come to me. She finally did, and it was the best hug I've ever had in my entire life. I still remember it. The love I felt from that little girl was unimaginable.

Chapter 22

OUTPATIENT REHAB BEGINS

One of the first things they do in outpatient treatment is a work-up evaluation. In that evaluation, I was diagnosed with bipolar I disorder. A lot of times, mental illness and drug addiction go hand in hand. It is called *dual diagnosis*. That was the first time in my entire life I had ever been diagnosed with bipolar disorder. Things started to make a little more sense to me at this point. Had I been self-medicating for all these years and never knew it?

For the next nine months, I attended meetings, got random drug tests, and worked hard on myself, while also being properly medicated. I passed through outpatient treatment and graduated, fulfilling all of my requirements.

Chapter 23

LIFE AFTER OUTPATIENT

For the following five years, I was on parole and probation. I had to see my probation officer monthly and do drug testing. During that time, I also had to do forty hours of community service and start paying restitution. I did everything I had to do because my freedom was on the line. One mistake, and I was going to be sent upstate for five years. That was not an option for me. I was not willing to ever be sent to jail again. I had worked too hard to get where I was.

During this time, I was talking to Jason. However, he was still actively using, so I would not go and hang out with him. Sadly, this disease took him a few years ago.

Chapter 24
RECOVERY

I attended Narcotics Anonymous and Alcoholics Anonymous meetings, got a sponsor, and did the 12 steps. I rebuilt my life from the bottom up. There were three things that were key to me: forgiveness, hope, and surrender. I had to first forgive myself before anyone else would. I knew I could never give up hope.

Surrender was the hardest one for me. I gave everything over to my higher power, and for me, that is God. I realized that my own best thinking had taken me to rock-bottom, so to keep doing it my way would definitely not work. Enough was enough. I had to stop, and I needed to change.

In my recovery, people said positive affirmations that have stuck with me to this day. Some of them are "I can do this," "Never give up," "I have the power to change my story," and "Some of y'all be judging people who beat situations that would have broken y'all in pieces!" (my absolute favorite).

Remember, we do not become addicts overnight, and we were not going to get things right or get back everything we had lost overnight. Hell, even now, I am still getting things back that I had lost. It takes time, patience, and a lot of dedication. If I can do it, you can do it too. You just have to want it. You have to choose life over death.

Know you are worth it. Know someone loves you. Know you are beautiful inside and out. We have all lost someone to this disease—someone we knew or someone we did not really know at all. I am sure as I am writing these words that someone has just passed away in this horrible epidemic. You and I do not have to be next.

We all have a purpose. With everything I have been through, and all the lessons I have learned, do you think this is the end of my journey? Think again!

GLOSSARY

Awakening: An act or moment of becoming suddenly aware of something

Boosting: Stealing something, then selling it for cash

Boot: A device to prevent a vehicle from being moved

Boulevard: Wide street in a town or city

Bundle: A collection of things or quantity of material tied or wrapped up together

Clean: Sober

Coke: Cocaine

Commissary: Food store in a military, prison, or other institution

Community: Service an offender is required to do instead of going to prison

Cop: Buy

Dual diagnosis: Having both a mental disorder and an alcohol or drug problem

Dumpster: Large container for rubbish

El: An elevated train in Philadelphia finished on November 5, 1922

Endocarditis: Inflammation of the endocardium

FIR: Forensic intensive recovery—a substance abuse treatment.

Food stamps: Also known as SNAP benefits—vouchers issued by the state to those on low incomes, exchangeable for food

Free samples: Drugs given away by a dealer, usually when they receive new product and want to see how good or bad it is

Higher power: Sometimes refers to a Supreme Being or other conceptions of God

Kensington: Neighborhood in Philadelphia that is considered the largest open-air heroin and fentanyl market in the world

Kirkbride Center: Inpatient treatment center in Philadelphia

Methadone clinic: Dispensary of medications used for treatment of opiate dependence

NHS: Outpatient treatment center in Philadelphia

Oxy 80s: Oxycontin prolonged-release tablets

Paddy wagon: Police van

Pawn: To exchange an item for immediate cash

Recovery house: An intervention that is specifically designed to address a recovering person's need for a safe and healthy living environment

Restitution: Recompense for injury or loss

Roundhouse: Philadelphia police headquarters

Self-medicate: Administer medication to oneself without medical supervision and/or take alcohol or drugs to relieve stress or other conditions

Sell oneself: Get paid for having sex with someone

Shady: Of doubtful honesty or legality

Snorting: Inhaling a drug in powdered form up the nose

Sober house: Supportive, structured living conditions

Speedball: Mixture of cocaine and heroin

Sting operation: Complicated confidence game planned and
    executed with great care, especially as implemented by
    undercover agents to apprehend criminals

Welfare: Statutory procedure or social effort designed to
    promote the basic physical and material well-being of
    people in need

Works: Needles

Printed in the United States
by Baker & Taylor Publisher Services